Dear Parents:

Congratulations! Your child is taking the first steps on an exciting journey. The destination? Independent reading!

STEP INTO READING® will help your child get there. The program offers five steps to reading success. Each step includes fun stories and colorful art or photographs. In addition to original fiction and books with favorite characters, there are Step into Reading Non-Fiction Readers, Phonics Readers and Boxed Sets, Sticker Readers, and Comic Readers—a complete literacy program with something to interest every child.

Learning to Read, Step by Step!

Ready to Read   Preschool–Kindergarten
• big type and easy words • rhyme and rhythm • picture clues
For children who know the alphabet and are eager to begin reading.

Reading with Help   Preschool–Grade 1
• basic vocabulary • short sentences • simple stories
For children who recognize familiar words and sound out new words with help.

Reading on Your Own   Grades 1–3
• engaging characters • easy-to-follow plots • popular topics
For children who are ready to read on their own.

Reading Paragraphs   Grades 2–3
• challenging vocabulary • short paragraphs • exciting stories
For newly independent readers who read simple sentences with confidence.

Ready for Chapters   Grades 2–4
• chapters • longer paragraphs • full-color art
For children who want to take the plunge into chapter books but still like colorful pictures.

STEP INTO READING® is designed to give every child a successful reading experience. The grade levels are only guides; children will progress through the steps at their own speed, developing confidence in their reading.

Remember, a lifetime love of reading starts with a single step!

Rule the School!

by Shea Fontana

illustrated by Dario Brizuela

Random House 🏠 New York

Cheetah wanted to prove that
she was the fastest runner
at Super Hero High.

When the whistle blew, she
sprinted with her super-speed!

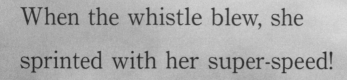

To make sure she would win,

Cheetah asked her friend, Frost,

to ice the track

so the other heroes would slip!

Cheetah's cheating didn't work.

She fell on the slippery ice

while Wonder Woman slid across

the finish line first!

Wonder Woman's friends cheered.

Cheetah was jealous.

Later, when Wonder Woman
returned a lost puppy to its owner,
everyone cheered for her again.
That made Cheetah more jealous!

8

"She's so popular! Why does
  everyone love her?" Cheetah asked Frost.
"That's easy," Frost replied.
"She's helpful and kind."

Cheetah had an idea.

She would rule the school

by becoming more popular

than Wonder Woman!

But being helpful and kind
was hard work. She decided it
would be easier to build friends.

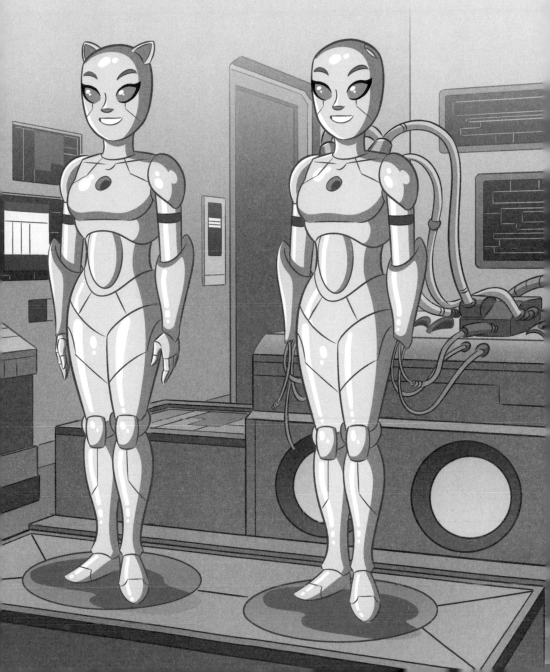

She made them
with metal and wires.
Then she dressed
them to be fabulous!

At Capes & Cowls Café,
Cheetah showed off her new friends.
They did whatever she wanted.

"That's a lot of gal pals!"
exclaimed Supergirl.
Wonder Woman wondered
who the new girls were.

Everyone loved Cheetah
and her new friends,
until she told one of her robots
to bring them smoothies.

She didn't think of what would
happen when her creations took a sip.
ZAP! ZAP! ZAP!
The robots sparked!

Instead of being friendly,
the robots began to wreck the café!
They broke tables and chairs
and scared the customers.

"Help!" cried Steve Trevor, who worked there. A robot poured a smoothie over his head. Cheetah had lost control!

She had to stop her creations,
and watching the heroes fight them
gave Cheetah an idea.
She told Wonder Woman
to fly out the door.

"Don't let her get away!"

Cheetah yelled.

She had programmed the robots

to compete with Wonder Woman.

She knew they would follow her.

Cheetah grabbed one end
of Wonder Woman's lasso.
She ran around the robots
at super-speed.

With Wonder Woman holding
the other end of the lasso,
the robots were soon tied up.

Dear Parents:

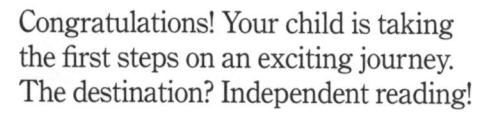

Congratulations! Your child is taking
the first steps on an exciting journey.
The destination? Independent reading!

STEP INTO READING® will help your child get there. The program offers
five steps to reading success. Each step includes fun stories and colorful
art or photographs. In addition to original fiction and books with favorite
characters, there are Step into Reading Non-Fiction Readers, Phonics Readers
and Boxed Sets, Sticker Readers, and Comic Readers—a complete literacy
program with something to interest every child.

Learning to Read, Step by Step!

Ready to Read   Preschool–Kindergarten
• big type and easy words • rhyme and rhythm • picture clues
For children who know the alphabet and are eager to
begin reading.

Reading with Help   Preschool–Grade 1
• basic vocabulary • short sentences • simple stories
For children who recognize familiar words and sound out
new words with help.

Reading on Your Own   Grades 1–3
• engaging characters • easy-to-follow plots • popular topics
For children who are ready to read on their own.

Reading Paragraphs   Grades 2–3
• challenging vocabulary • short paragraphs • exciting stories
For newly independent readers who read simple sentences
with confidence.

Ready for Chapters   Grades 2–4
• chapters • longer paragraphs • full-color art
For children who want to take the plunge into chapter books
but still like colorful pictures.

STEP INTO READING® is designed to give every child a successful
reading experience. The grade levels are only guides; children will progress
through the steps at their own speed, developing confidence in their reading.

Remember, a lifetime love of reading starts with a single step!

For Adam —S.F.

Copyright © 2018 DC Comics.
DC SUPER HERO GIRLS and all related characters
and elements © & ™ DC Comics and
Warner Bros. Entertainment Inc.
WB SHIELD: ™ & © WBEI (s18)
RHUS40094

Visit us on the Web!
StepIntoReading.com
rhcbooks.com
dcsuperherogirls.com
dckids.kidswb.com

Educators and librarians, for a variety of teaching tools, visit us at RHTeachersLibrarians.com

ISBN 978-0-525-57809-3 (trade) — ISBN 978-0-525-57810-9 (lib. bdg.) —
ISBN 978-0-525-57811-6 (ebook)

Printed in the United States of America
10 9 8 7 6 5 4 3 2 1

STEP 3
READING ON YOUR OWN

STEP INTO READING®

DC SuperHero Girls™

Wonder Woman ★ for President

by Shea Fontana

illustrated by Dario Brizuela

Random House 🏠 New York

It was time for student elections
at Super Hero High.

Wonder Woman was a natural leader.

She wanted to be class president.

5

Bumblebee talked to the students about what the new president could do for Super Hero High. And Harley was in charge of the fun!

Supergirl handed out flyers

to the school's fliers.

They were sure

Wonder Woman could win!

But Cheetah and Miss Martian
were also in the race.

They were working hard to win, too.
Cheetah gave out fun cat ears.

Miss Martian listened to the younger
students.

As the candidates for class president
rehearsed their speeches,
Wonder Woman heard a loud noise!
Miss Martian looked up—

It was the Female Furies!
These super-villains from Apokolips
wanted to cause chaos at
Super Hero High's election.

"Stop them!" said Wonder Woman.
She and Cheetah charged toward
Lashina and Speed Queen.

Miss Martian was so startled
that she became invisible.
It always happened
when she was scared.

Wonder Woman was shocked
by the tip of Lashina's
electric whip,
making it hard to fight back.

Cheetah raced after Speed Queen,
but the villain's skates spewed
a cloud of stinky gas.
Cheetah gasped.

The Furies trapped Wonder Woman
and Cheetah in a force field!
"Now we wreck the school,"
said Lashina.

When the Furies left,
Miss Martian became visible
and freed her friends.

Wonder Woman had a plan.
Miss Martian snuck ahead
of Speed Queen and poured
soapy water in her way.

Then Cheetah pounced on Lashina,
sending her stumbling.
Wonder Woman lassoed
the angry villain.

The heroes had saved the day

and the election.

After Wonder Woman flew

the Furies to the police station,

the Super Hero High students voted.

"Wonder Woman is president!"
announced Principal Waller.
But Wonder Woman knew
she hadn't done it alone.

Wonder Woman invited Cheetah
and Miss Martian to help her
fulfill her duties.
Together, they would be
a super team of leaders!

Everyone cheered for Cheetah
and Wonder Woman!
Cheetah realized that
the way to make real friends
was to be a good friend.